Francis Frith's

Around
Bedford

Photographic Memories

Francis Frith's

Around
Bedford

Martin Andrew

First published in the United Kingdom in 2001 by
Frith Book Company Ltd

Paperback Edition 2001
ISBN 1-85937-205-8

Hardback Edition 2001
ISBN 1-85937-348-8

British Library Cataloguing in Publication Data

Francis Frith's Bedford
Martin Andrew

Frith Book Company Ltd
Frith's Barn, Teffont,
Salisbury, Wiltshire SP3 5QP
Tel: +44 (0) 1722 716 376
Email: info@frithbook.co.uk
www.frithbook.co.uk

Printed and bound in Great Britain

Front Cover: Bedford, High Street 1921 70423

Contents

Francis Frith: Victorian Pioneer   7

Frith's Archive - A Unique Legacy   10

Bradford - An Introduction   12

Public Buildings & Schools   18

Bedford on the River Ouse   24

A walk through Bedford   47

A Tour to the West of Bedford   71

A Tour to the East of Bedford   79

Index   87

Free Mounted Print Voucher   91

Francis Frith: *Victorian Pioneer*

FRANCIS FRITH, Victorian founder of the world-famous photographic archive, was a complex and multi-talented man. A devout Quaker and a highly successful Victorian businessman, he was both philosophic by nature and pioneering in outlook.

By 1855 Francis Frith had already established a wholesale grocery business in Liverpool, and sold it for the astonishing sum of £200,000, which is the equivalent today of over £15,000,000. Now a multi-millionaire, he was able to indulge his passion for travel. As a child he had pored over travel books written by early explorers, and his fancy and imagination had been stirred by family holidays to the sublime mountain regions of Wales and Scotland. 'What a land of spirit-stirring and enriching scenes and places!' he had written. He was to return to these scenes of grandeur in later years to 'recapture the thousands of vivid and tender memories', but with a different purpose. Now in his thirties, and captivated by the new science of photography, Frith set out on a series of pioneering journeys to the Nile regions that occupied him from 1856 until 1860.

Intrigue and Adventure

He took with him on his travels a specially-designed wicker carriage that acted as both dark-room and sleeping chamber. These far-flung journeys were packed with intrigue and adventure. In his life story, written when he was sixty-three, Frith tells of being held captive by bandits, and of fighting 'an awful midnight battle to the very point of surrender with a deadly pack of hungry, wild dogs'. Sporting flowing Arab costume, Frith arrived at Akaba by camel seventy years before Lawrence, where he encountered 'desert princes and rival sheikhs, blazing with jewel-hilted swords'.

During these extraordinary adventures he was assiduously exploring the desert regions bordering the Nile and patiently recording the antiquities and peoples with his camera. He was the first photographer to venture beyond the sixth cataract. Africa was still the mysterious 'Dark Continent', and Stanley and Livingstone's historic meeting was a decade into the future. The conditions for picture taking confound belief. He laboured for hours in his wicker dark-room in the sweltering heat of the desert, while the volatile chemicals fizzed dangerously in their trays. Often he was forced to work in remote tombs and caves where conditions were cooler. Back in London he exhibited his photographs and was 'rapturously cheered' by members of the Royal Society. His reputation as a photographer was made overnight. An eminent modern historian has likened their impact on the population of the time to that on our own generation of the first photographs taken on the surface of the moon.

Venture of a Life-Time

Characteristically, Frith quickly spotted the opportunity to create a new business as a specialist publisher of photographs. He lived in an era of immense and sometimes violent change. For the poor in the early part of Victoria's reign work was a drudge and the hours long, and people had precious little free time to enjoy themselves. Most had no transport other than a cart or gig at their disposal, and had not travelled far beyond the boundaries of their own town or village. However,

by the 1870s, the railways had threaded their way across the country, and Bank Holidays and half-day Saturdays had been made obligatory by Act of Parliament. All of a sudden the ordinary working man and his family were able to enjoy days out and see a little more of the world.

With characteristic business acumen, Francis Frith foresaw that these new tourists would enjoy having souvenirs to commemorate their days out. In 1860 he married Mary Ann Rosling and set out with the intention of photographing every city, town and village in Britain. For the next thirty years he travelled the country by train and by pony and trap, producing fine photographs of seaside resorts and beauty spots that were keenly bought by millions of Victorians. These prints were painstakingly pasted into family albums and pored over during the dark nights of winter, rekindling precious memories of summer excursions.

The Rise of Frith & Co

Frith's studio was soon supplying retail shops all over the country. To meet the demand he gathered about him a small team of photographers, and published the work of independent artist-photographers of the calibre of Roger Fenton and Francis Bedford. In order to gain some understanding of the scale of Frith's business one only has to look at the catalogue issued by Frith & Co in 1886: it runs to some 670 pages, listing not only many thousands of views of the British Isles but also many photographs of most European countries, and China, Japan, the USA and Canada — note the sample page shown above from the hand-written *Frith & Co* ledgers detailing pictures taken. By 1890 Frith had created the greatest specialist photographic publishing company in the world,

Frith's death, a new card measuring 5.5 x 3.5 inches became the standard format, but it was not until 1902 that the divided back came into being, with address and message on one face and a full-size illustration on the other. *Frith & Co* were in the vanguard of postcard development, and Frith's sons Eustace and Cyril continued their father's monumental task, expanding the number of views offered to the public and recording more and more places in Britain, as the coasts and countryside were opened up to mass travel.

Francis Frith died in 1898 at his villa in Cannes, his great project still growing. The archive he created continued in business for another seventy years. By 1970 it contained over a third of a million pictures of 7,000 cities, towns and villages. The massive photographic record Frith has left to us stands as a living monument to a special and very remarkable man.

with over 2,000 outlets – more than the combined number that Boots and W H Smith have today! The picture on the right shows the *Frith & Co* display board at Ingleton in the Yorkshire Dales. Beautifully constructed with mahogany frame and gilt inserts, it could display up to a dozen local scenes.

Postcard Bonanza

The ever-popular holiday postcard we know today took many years to develop. In 1870 the Post Office issued the first plain cards, with a pre-printed stamp on one face. In 1894 they allowed other publishers' cards to be sent through the mail with an attached adhesive halfpenny stamp. Demand grew rapidly, and in 1895 a new size of postcard was permitted called the court card, but there was little room for illustration. In 1899, a year after

Frith's Archive: *A Unique Legacy*

FRANCIS FRITH'S legacy to us today is of immense significance and value, for the magnificent archive of evocative photographs he created provides a unique record of change in 7,000 cities, towns and villages throughout Britain over a century and more. Frith and his fellow studio photographers revisited locations many times down the years to update their views, compiling for us an enthralling and colourful pageant of British life and character.

We tend to think of Frith's sepia views of Britain as nostalgic, for most of us use them to conjure up memories of places in our own lives with which we have family associations. It often makes us forget that to Francis Frith they were records of daily life as it was actually being lived in the cities, towns and villages of his day. The Victorian age was one of great and often bewildering change for ordinary people, and though the pictures evoke an impression of slower times, life was as busy and hectic as it is today.

We are fortunate that Frith was a photographer of the people, dedicated to recording the minutiae of everyday life. For it is this sheer wealth of visual data, the painstaking chronicle of changes in dress, transport, street layouts, buildings, housing, engineering and landscape that captivates us so much today. His remarkable images offer us a powerful link with the past and with the lives of our ancestors.

Today's Technology

Computers have now made it possible for Frith's many thousands of images to be accessed almost instantly. In the Frith archive today, each photograph is carefully 'digitised' then stored on a CD Rom. Frith archivists can locate a single photograph amongst thousands within seconds. Views can be catalogued and sorted under a variety of categories of place and content to the immediate benefit of researchers.

Inexpensive reference prints can be created for them at the touch of a mouse button, and a wide range of books and other printed materials assembled and published for a wider, more general readership - in the next twelve months over a hundred Frith local history titles will be published! The day-to-day workings of the archive are very different from how they were in Francis Frith's time: imagine the herculean task of sorting through eleven tons of glass negatives as Frith had to do to locate a particular sequence of pictures! Yet

See Frith at www. frithbook.co.uk

the archive still prides itself on maintaining the same high standards of excellence laid down by Francis Frith, including the painstaking cataloguing and indexing of every view.

It is curious to reflect on how the internet now allows researchers in America and elsewhere greater instant access to the archive than Frith himself ever enjoyed. Many thousands of individual views can be called up on screen within seconds on one of the Frith internet sites, enabling people living continents away to revisit the streets of their ancestral home town, or view places in Britain where they have enjoyed holidays. Many overseas researchers welcome the chance to view special theme selections, such as transport, sports, costume and ancient monuments.

We are certain that Francis Frith would have heartily approved of these modern developments in imaging techniques, for he himself was always working at the very limits of Victorian photographic technology.

The Value of the Archive Today

Because of the benefits brought by the computer, Frith's images are increasingly studied by social historians, by researchers into genealogy and ancestory, by architects, town planners, and by teachers and schoolchildren involved in local history projects.

In addition, the archive offers every one of us an opportunity to examine the places where we and our families have lived and worked down the years. Highly successful in Frith's own era, the archive is now, a century and more on, entering a new phase of popularity.

The Past in Tune with the Future

Historians consider the Francis Frith Collection to be of prime national importance. It is the only archive of its kind remaining in private ownership and has been valued at a million pounds. However, this figure is now rapidly increasing as digital technology enables more and more people around the world to enjoy its benefits.

Francis Frith's archive is now housed in an historic timber barn in the beautiful village of Teffont in Wiltshire. Its founder would not recognize the archive office as it is today. In place of the many thousands of dusty boxes containing glass plate negatives and an all-pervading odour of photographic chemicals, there are now ranks of computer screens. He would be amazed to watch his images travelling round the world at unimaginable speeds through network and internet lines.

The archive's future is both bright and exciting. Francis Frith, with his unshakeable belief in making photographs available to the greatest number of people, would undoubtedly approve of what is being done today with his lifetime's work. His photographs, depicting our shared past, are now bringing pleasure and enlightenment to millions around the world a century and more after his death.

Bedford - *An Introduction*

UNTIL THE MID 18th century Bedford was a remarkably compact town, little more than two thirds of a mile from north to south and a quarter of a mile wide at various points. Bedford had, like most English towns, a relatively small population. In the 1670s it was about 2,150, and by 1800 it had increased to nearer 3,000. That is the population of a largish village nowadays; yet that population was sufficient to sustain five parish churches and a number of Nonconformist congregations. Nowadays a population that small would barely support a parish church and a village shop. The town expanded considerably in the 19th century, a growth reflected in the population figures: these increased from 6,959 in the 1831 census to 16,850 in 1871 and 39,183 by 1911. The population has since doubled; the town has

expanded in most directions, but particularly to the east, absorbing the village of Goldington and large acreages of farmland. However, despite all this change, the historic core around the Ouse bridge is still recognisable, and the town is a pleasant one to visit.

There have been architectural and planning disasters in Bedford, and that great god the internal combustion engine has been propitiated rather too readily in the last forty years. Architecturally there have been some sad losses: these include some of the old inns, such as the part-medieval George Inn and the White Horse, while the old town south of the river has suffered most. Modern buildings have often been ill-judged and aggressive: it is difficult to forgive the Moat House Hotel on the south bank of the Ouse by the bridge, a monstrous fourteen-storey concrete carbuncle that is an insult to the river and the town. However, enough survives to help us catch much of the flavour of this ancient county town - but to do so we must walk, not drive. The core is small enough to make this an attractive option: Chapters 2 and 3 are in the form of two pedestrian routes, one alongside the Ouse as it passes through the town, the other a walk from south of the river through the town northwards to finish in Bedford Park, a mile or so from north to south.

Although there have been finds of Roman material such as coins, there is little evidence of any substantial settlement before the Anglo-Saxons arrived in the 5th century AD, although there was apparently a Romano-British community at nearby Kempston. The name of the town tells it all: Beda's ford across the Ouse, Beda presumably being an Anglo-Saxon leader who settled here on the north bank. When the Danes invaded in the 9th century, the country was eventually divided up at the Treaty of Wedmore in 886 AD between King Alfred's Wessex and English Mercia and the Danelaw to the north-east. The Ouse formed part of the agreed boundary: Bedford was under Danish rule as part of the Danish Guthrum's kingdom, while south of the Ouse was English territory.

In the midst of these turbulent years of Anglo-Danish struggle, Bedford springs into written history in 'The Anglo-Saxon Chronicle', that vivid and extraordinary contemporary record of English history as it unfolded up to 1154. Under the entry for the year 918 AD, during King Edward the Elder's systematic reconquest of the Danish areas, it records that 'Jarl Thurcytel submitted to him and all the Danish barons, and almost all the chief men who owed allegiance to Bedford'. In November 919 AD 'King Edward went with his army to Bedford and occupied the fortress: most of the garrison who had previously occupied it submitted to him. He remained there for four weeks, and before he left he ordered the fortress on the south bank of the river to be built'. Thus Bedford assumed its medieval shape on both sides of the river; indeed, part of the King's Ditch, built for Edward, still remains filled with water, but the stockades have long gone. All was not sweetness and light thereafter. Under 921 AD, the Anglo-Saxon Chronicle records that a marauding Danish army reached Bedford having ravaged the Huntingdon area; 'the [Bedford] garrison sallied out to meet them, fought against them and put them to flight, slaying a good part of them'. These entries are of great interest, for they show that the town existed well before 918 AD and that it was well fortified; more crucially, the entries give a precise date for the southern expansion of the town.

When administrative areas were set up after the English re-conquest, Bedford was important enough to be selected as the chief town of the new

shire, Bedfordshire. In the 11th century the town prospered as a trading centre as well, and even minted its own coins. Architectural evidence of the pre-Norman town is scanty but significant: it includes the present chancel of St Peter de Merton, and some re-used stones and walling in St Mary's south of the river. (St Cuthbert is an Anglo-Saxon dedication, but the medieval church was rebuilt in the 1840s). After the Norman Conquest, the town underwent a radical change: the south-east part of the north bank town was cleared to make way for a large castle with a motte and the bailey, which extended to St Paul's Square. The motte, or castle mound, survives to the north of the little park at Castle Close, and there is some 12th-century masonry still to be seen. It saw action during the Civil Wars of King Stephen's reign - there were sieges in 1137, 1141 and in 1153, when Henry, later King Henry II, captured it and the town; after plundering it, he 'delivered it to the flames'.

More peacefully, the rebuilt town received a Royal charter from Henry II, now king, in 1166; this confirmed the town's market and trading rights which had been granted by Henry I some years before. By 1200, Bedford had a river bridge with a nearby chapel, a hospital, St John's (south of the river and founded by Robert de Parys, and still retaining its early 13th-century structure), a county gaol, and two monasteries outside the town, Newnham Priory to the east and Caldwell

Priory in Kempston parish. Nearby to the south was the Norman foundation of Elstow Abbey. Within the town there were now several parishes, as befitted a county town: St Peter de Dunstable, St Mary, and St John south of the river, the last in effect the chapel to St John's Hospital. To the north of the river were the main church of St Paul, St Peter de Merton, and St Cuthbert, besides the bridge chapel and the Herne Chapel. During the 13th century the town acquired a Franciscan Friary (1238) and a leper hospital, St Leonard's Hospital, just outside the southern part of town on the Ampthill road.

The castle endured its last siege in 1224 when the young king, Henry III, was outraged by the seizure of one of his judges, Henry de Braybrooke, by the castellan, the over-mighty subject par excellence, Falkes de Breaute. The siege was described in lingering detail by a bloodthirsty monk at Dunstable Priory, and is one of the best contemporary sources for a medieval siege. It lasted eight weeks, and included the excommunication of the garrison by the Archbishop of Canterbury during the siege and their hanging afterwards. The castle was slighted, and some of the stonework was used in repairs to St Paul's church and other Bedford buildings.

What remains now of medieval Bedford? The churches survive in various degrees of authenticity, apart from St Cuthbert's, which was rebuilt entirely in the 1840s; some of St John's

Hospital also survives, and so do other fragments. The stone bridge, which was probably repaired with castle stone after 1224, and which originally dated from the later 12th century, was replaced in the 19th century, and the part-medieval George Inn off the High Street was also demolished.

During Tudor times the prosperous market and county town saw two major developments that had a profound effect on the town's future: one was the rise of Protestantism and the closure of the religious houses, and the other was the endowment of a school by Sir William Harpur. The religious houses were closed by the Dissolution of the Monasteries under Henry VIII: Caldwell Priory in 1536, the Friary in 1538, Elstow Abbey (where the laxity and luxurious life-style of the nuns was somewhat notorious) in 1539 and Newnham in 1541. St John's Hospital survived as a type of almshouse. Puritans and Calvinists are recorded from the middle of the century, but this had more impact in the following century.

Of greater long-term and continuing significance was Sir William Harpur and his wife Dame Alice's endowment of a school in 1566. Harpur had been Lord Mayor of London in 1561; he gave land in Holborn, whose income was to fund the school, and any surplus was to go to the poor of Bedford. The income turned out to be considerable, and the Harpur endowment prospered over the centuries. A new Harpur Trust was set up in 1764 which worked in collaboration with the town over succeeding years. It funded several schools, such as Bedford School itself, Bedford High School and the Harpur Schools in Harpur Street, as well as funding other charity work and almshouses, such as those in Dame Alice Street of 1801-06. For many years the Harpur Trust was in effect the provider of virtually all education in Bedford. Its role cannot be over-emphasised in the shaping of the town. Sir William died in 1573; his brass and that to Dame Alice is in St Paul's Church. More oddly, there is a statue of him in a niche in the facade of the former school in St Paul's Square, which was built in 1756 (it is now the Town Hall). This statue shows him dressed in 18th-century clothes, rather than in Tudor ones!

In the 17th century, Bedford was staunchly Parliamentarian during the Civil War. A soldier in the Parliamentary garrison at Newport Pagnell was an Elstow man, one John Bunyan. After the war he moved to Bedford, and sought spiritual help from John Gifford, the Puritan vicar of St John's Church, as a plaque informs us. The Independents prospered, but Bunyan was imprisoned in 1660. While he was in Bedford Gaol he wrote 'Grace Abounding' in 1666, and started work on 'The Pilgrim's Progress'. Released in 1672, and now Pastor of the Independents, he was again imprisoned, this time for not taking Church of England communion; he finished 'The Pilgrim's Progress' in 1678. He wrote much more, but this

book fired the public imagination; it remained very widely read until well into the 20th century.

Bedford continued to do well as a trading town: Daniel Defoe described it as 'a large, populous, well-built and thriving town'. The river was made navigable in the 1680s, and wharves and warehouses and stores appeared. Coal, fish brought up-river in perforated metal trunks towed behind the barges, salt, millstones, tar, iron, timber and brick were landed at the wharves, while mainly agricultural produce such as wheat, malt, beans and apples in season were loaded for transport down-river. Coal was the main import in the 18th century, and brewing grew in importance as an industry.

The Dukes of Bedford became steadily more influential in the town's affairs. Their great estate was at Woburn, and they owned land all over the county and in London, some of it in Bloomsbury quite near the Holborn estate owned by the Harpur foundation. Thus the Dukes saw the mismanagement of the Harpur endowment by the town corporation at close hand; the Harpur Trust was set up in 1764 to administer better the Tudor endowment and its income. The story of the Trust from the later 18th century onwards is one of increased educational provision for the children of the town and, by the introduction of boarding, for children from further away. Indeed, in the 19th century large numbers of children of officials of the East India Company and the subsequent government of India were boarded in Bedford School and at other schools with boarding facilities. Some of these school buildings are seen in Chapter 1.

The town also began to acquire other public buildings and facilities in this period, including the House of Industry on the Kimbolton Road, later converted to a workhouse. In 1801 the much-needed rebuilding of the old typhus-infested Gaol was achieved, and on the Ampthill Road an Infirmary was built in 1803 and a lunatic asylum nearby in 1811. In 1803 a private Act of Parliament set up Improvement Commissioners; they eventually had the new bridge built and opened in 1813, and cleared away squalid tenements from St Paul's Square. The railway arrived in 1846; then in 1862 the Bedford to Cambridge line was opened, and in 1872 a line to Northampton.

Later in the 19th century, the new Corn Exchange was opened in 1874. In the 1880s, during the vigorous mayoralty of Joshua Hawkins, the river banks east of the bridge were converted into parks, the Suspension Bridge was built, and Bedford Park was laid out; virtually everything was opened by the Duke of Bedford or his sons. In the 20th century the industrial riverside disappeared, and more parks and walkways were developed along the western part of the river, including St Mary's Park on the south bank, while the north bank walkway has only recently been completed.

After World War II there was considerable destruction and demolition in the name of progress, and much of the old town south of the river was seriously compromised. However, the tide has now turned, and there is greater appreciation of what gives a town its distinctive character. For example, the Harpur Schools in Harpur Street, seen in view 39933 in Chapter 1, were kept as the frontage block to a new shopping centre in the 1990s: this would not have happened in the gung-ho 1960s, when site clearance was the norm in any development.

On a sunny summer's day or a brisk autumn one, the riverside parks are a delight; they and Bedford Park itself are immensely popular still. The townscape is rewarding, with St Paul's Square and St Peter's Green the highlights. The historic core is, as I wrote earlier, not large by any means, and merits a day's wandering around. I have divided the town tour into two: a walk along the banks of the River Ouse, perhaps the town's greatest asset, in Chapter 2, and a stroll from south to north through the town centre in Chapter 3. The last two chapters are brief tours of parts of Bedfordshire which in terms of Chapter 5 should point up the virtues of Bedford compared with the eastern towns along the A1 and nearby - Shefford, Biggleswade and Sandy. The first chapter looks at some of the major civic and educational buildings to set the scene. I hope you enjoy the selection: I was certainly fortunate in having a brilliant sunny late autumn day for walking the riverside chapter.

Public Buildings & Schools

Bedford School, The Sports Fields 1921 71431

The Town Hall 1897 39930
The Town Hall, on the west side of St Paul's Square, started life as a school, a school originally founded by Sir William Harpur (a key name in Bedford's history) in 1566. The left-hand part was the school, rebuilt in 1756 with a statue of Harpur in a niche. The porch with the turret and the parts to its right were added in 1860 by a local architect, James Horsford, and is now the Bedford Civic Theatre. Behind is now the 1960s council offices, a seven-storey block.

◄ **The Harpur Schools 1897**
39933
In the far distance is the old Harpur School, now the Town Hall. It was supplemented by this fine Tudor-style battlemented building when the Harpur Trust built the Modern School, or the Harpur Schools, in the 1830s; the building was designed by the renowned local architect John Wing, whose son was a pupil, but was completed by John Blore. No longer a school, it was preserved as a frontage to a shopping centre. The railings have long gone, but two of the ornate cast-iron lamp-posts survive in what is now a pedestrianised street.

◀ **The Corn Exchange 1897** 39931

On the north side of St Paul's Square is the old corn exchange, an uncompromisingly Victorian building whose foundation stone was laid in October 1872. Another stone plaque commemorates its opening in April 1874 by the then Duke of Bedford. It replaced a Corn Exchange of 1849 which had proved too small; it then became the Floral Hall. Now a plaque and bust commemorate the fact that Glenn Miller and his orchestra played here during World War II.

▼ **Bedford Grammar School 1897** 39935

Our look at the fine schools of Bedford moves north beyond St Peter's Square to Bedford School. This had its origins in the free school founded by Sir William Harpur in 1566. The Harpur Trust, following the decay of its school in the 18th century, made ample amends in the 19th with the Harpur Schools in the 1830s; then after 1873 it had three further schools built. Here we see the south front of the grammar school; it is now Bedford School, and from the start took boarders as well as day boys.

◀ **Bedford Grammar School 1898** 40859

In 1898 the school buildings were still crisp and new; they show well the Gothic Revival style chosen by Robins - this style was favoured by schools in Victorian times. The north front, seen here, is the best elevation, with its central turret flanked by Gothic traceried windows and battlements. Above is a louvred turret with a spirelet. The only post-medieval feature is the Georgian dormers in the steep roof. The school is an undoubted success, and a great asset to the town.

◄ **The Girls' School 1897** 39934
Now Bedford High School for Girls, this fine building originally housed both the High School and the girls' Modern School. Opened in 1882, it was designed by the leading architect Basil Champneys in a Jacobethan style, with numerous shaped gables and mullioned and transomed windows. The Modern School moved out in 1892. This east front faces the high walls surrounding Bedford Prison on the other side of Adelaide Square, which is itself a collection of fine buildings, some of 1801 by Bedford's own John Wing.

◄ Bedford School, The Sports Fields 1921 70431

The grammar school moved out of its old buildings (now the Town Hall) to a new twenty-acre site set in fields north of St Peter's church in 1891. In this view we look south past cricket games towards the main buildings of 1889-1892. To their left a science block was added in 1933; there is a chapel further to the left, designed in 1909 by Bodley. To the right are the back garden walls of the villas in De Parys Avenue.

▼ The County Schools 1897

39936

South-west of the town centre, along the Ampthill Road, on a large site between it and the railway line, the County Schools were built in the 1880s on a grand plan with a massive tower and, to the left, a fine chapel. Long demolished, its site is now occupied by Technology House, a rather good 1960s building, long and well-proportioned and in generous grounds, the remnants of the school site.

◄ The Infirmary 1897 39937

The old Infirmary, designed by John Wing and opened in 1803, fronted Ampthill Road; it was later expanded to be the Bedford General Hospital (South Site). Founded with a bequest from Samuel Whitbread, it had fifty beds - and a budget of £50 a year for leeches. In 1899, two years after this view was taken, it was replaced by fiery red brick and terra cotta buildings; its site is now occupied by an uninspiring Accident and Emergency building opened in 1964. It is a sad loss to the architectural heritage of the town.

Bedford on the River Ouse

Stone Bridge from St Mary's Gardens 1897 39957

On the Ouse 1897 39953
Bedford grew up at a ford over the River Ouse before the arrival of the Anglo-Saxons in the mid to late 5th century AD. It is certainly the river that gives the town its character now. It is probably its greatest asset. Its banks are laid out for parks and walks; they are very popular for walking, and are a-throng on a sunny summer or winter weekend. The river rises on the Northamptonshire-Oxfordshire border and winds east through Bedford on its leisurely way to the Wash near King's Lynn.

Stone Bridge from St Mary's Gardens 1897 39957
The medieval river bridge was replaced by the Improvement
Commissioners set up by Act of Parliament in 1803. Besides being
empowered to replace the bridge, they cleared away numerous
houses near St Peter's Church and the medieval Guildhall in their
zeal - no doubt the area was in serious decay. Perhaps those
staying at the elegant Swan Hotel by the river brought pressure on
the town to clear its riverside slums.

The Swan Hotel and the River 1898 40862
Highway improvements have swept away the Italianate and balustraded mid 19th-century buildings in front of the spire, which is that of St Paul's Church. At the far right is the Swan Hotel. This elegant stone building was designed by Henry Holland and built in 1794, replacing an earlier timber-framed inn nearer the bridge. Holland had worked for the Duke of Bedford at his seat at Woburn Abbey some ten miles south-west of Bedford, and the duke had acquired the old inn in 1787.

The Bridge 1921 70434
The present bridge was designed by the local architect John Wing. Its foundation stone was laid by the Marquess of Tavistock, the eldest son of the Duke of Bedford, in 1811. The costs proved high. By the time the bridge opened in November 1813, it was done without ceremony: the local MP, Samuel Whitbread, merely walked across to meet the Commissioners and shake hands. A further plaque records that it was opened free of tolls in 1835 - the debt by then had been paid off.

▼ **The Bridge 1921** 70433
The south bank was a popular location for hiring rowing boats, and the Bedford Rowing Club, founded in 1886, have their boat and club house to the left of the photographer. To the left, behind the bridge are the chimneys of Alfred Waterhouse's fiery red brick and terra cotta former Shire Hall, dated 1881, with its main front to St Peter's Square. The tall works chimney has long gone.

▼ **The Bridge 1921** 70432
John Wing's 1811 bridge replaced a medieval one built or rebuilt soon after 1224; the builders probably used stone from the demolished castle, which was destroyed or 'slighted' after a punishing siege in that year. There was a chapel on an earlier bridge by 1194, when it was granted to Bedford's St John's Hospital along with the bridge alms and tolls. A similar bridge chapel survives at St Ives further downstream.

▲ **The River 1921** 70435
This view looks across the river to the south bank, now a much changed view. The Picturedrome at this time was showing 'Madame Peacock' daily at 3, 7 and 9 o'clock. To its left and out of view are the late 1880s gables of the Bedford Rowing Club. This view is now marred, to put it mildly, by the concrete eyesore of the Moat House Hotel, 14 storeys of 1960s aggression: but there are good views from the rooms, no doubt.

◄ **The River and the Bridge c1960** B51086
This view gives more of a modern feel. The buildings on Vines Corner to the left of the bridge have gone, while Swan House to the left of Holland's dignified Swan Hotel replaced the house and shops seen in photograph No B51054; they were demolished in 1960 to make way for the present building. The demolition of Vines Corner opened up St Paul's Square by destroying a key element of its south side.

◀ **The Promenade 1897**
39947
In this view, looking north-west from the bridge on the south bank of the Ouse, the Swan Hotel is seen without ivy. The pediment on the lef is that of the main west elevation facing the town: the graceful columned portico can be glimpsed through the trees. It was from this court, formed by the demolition of the old Swan Inn, that coaches left for London and other towns until the mid 1850s.

◀ The Bridge over the Ouse c1960 B51054

This view was taken from near the Bedford Rowing Club clubhouse just before the buildings on the right were demolished for Swan House in 1960. Centre right, the white gable was hidden by Vines Corner, seen in view 70432. There is some townscape benefit in seeing more of St Paul's Church spire and tower, I suppose. To the left is Waterhouse's former Shire Hall, now arcaded at ground level for a riverside walk.

▼ The River Ouse 1929

81733

Another glimpse of the Swan Hotel's neo-classical portico can be seen through the leaves on the left. The views of the river from the principal bedrooms of the hotel were described by the diarist John Byng in the late 1790s as being highly agreeable with 'the smoothness of the wide water, the skipping of the fish, and the sight of a party of elegant female rowers'.

◀ The Embankment 1921 70437

Several of Frith's 1921 views of the river have the same river launch loitering in the foreground (compare with 70432, 70435 and 81732, a return visit by the same photographer in 1929?). In this view, taken from the bridge, the trees obscure the tall two-gabled building of 1885 beyond the Swan Hotel. It was built as the Town and Country Club by the architect Henry Cheers; it later became the County Library, before disappearing in the 1950s to make way for additions to the hotel.

The View from the Bridge c1955 B51040
Taken from slightly further out over the river from the bridge, this view shows the riverside conservatory/orangery added to the Swan's rear ranges before 1900 - it has subsequently been reconstructed. The high brick walls beyond belong to the 1885 Town and Country Club, later a library, which was swept away for the present twelve-bay, three-storey hotel bedroom wing in the 1950s.

◄ The River Ouse c1955 B51041
Taken from the bridge, this view looks along a busy Embankment to Embankment Gardens in the distance with its tree-lined river bank. The south bank is a series of islands linked by footbridges, and is just as popular as public parkland. Commerce was upstream of the bridge, behind the photographer, where the banks were lined with wharves.

▼ The River Ouse c1965
B51124
We are looking south-east from the Embankment. The river basks in afternoon sunshine, with swans and a hired rowing boat on the water. Immediately to the right of the inlet is the Bedford Rowing Club's clubhouse; further right, by the bridge, the Moat House 1960s tower block is mercifully out of shot. The south bank's islands (there is a back river beyond) are mostly lined by willow trees.

◄ The River 1929 81728
We have now moved upstream west of the bridge, with a view taken from St Mary's Embankment in St Mary's Gardens. These had been opened in 1923 following the clearance of the wharves and warehouses; the river had become a leisure amenity rather than a commercial highway. Opposite are the Shire Hall on the right and council offices on the left - until 1880 Bernards Wharves were on the site. The warehouse on the far right has now been demolished.

▼ The River 1929 81732

Further west, this view is taken from the Prebend Street Bridge on the south side of the tree-covered eyot in the middle of the river. The bridge was opened in October 1884 during the mayoralty of the indefatigable Joshua Hawkins. This is recorded on a plaque reused when the bridge was entirely rebuilt in 1992 and formally reopened by the Lord Lieutenant, Samuel Whitbread: a neat symmetry, for his ancestor, also Samuel, had opened the main bridge in 1813.

▼ The Suspension Bridge 1898 40864

We now return downstream beyond the 1813 Ouse bridge to the Embankment area, and to the parks and gardens mostly laid out during Joshua Hawkins' mayoralty in the 1880s. The parks and river walks are wonderful assets for the townspeople, and are still as popular as when they were first laid out. Crucial to Hawkins' plans was the linking of the south and north banks: this graceful suspension bridge, designed by John Webster and built in 1888, achieved this.

The Promenade 1897

39948

On the north bank, Embankment Gardens were laid out in the late 1880s with wide tree-lined walks along the river bank. There are ornamental flower beds amid grass between the walks and The Embankment road, which curves away from the river to accommodate the park before coming closer to the river near the Suspension Bridge. To the north of The Embankment, prosperous 1890s villas were built, most of which survive unchanged.

▼ **On the Ouse 1897** 39958

The south bank always remained less formal than the north; it is a series of islands separated from the 'mainland' by a back river, which in its turn is separated by weirs from the north river. Here we see boys fishing in the backwater, the edges reed-girt. These waters drove a number of watermills, such as Duck Mill and Newnham Mill, now vanished; some of them dated back to the Middle Ages.

▼ **A Waterfall on the Ouse 1897** 39959

In this view the photographer is looking north from the 'mainland' bank to the bridge, Boatslide Weir Bridge, which links Mill Meadows Island with Longholme. Beyond the weir is the main river and the trees along the north bank of the Ouse. The bridge in the photograph was less than ten years old at the time of the photograph; it has recently been reconstructed, with plain timber balustrades replacing the rustic 1880s ones.

▲ **The Lower River and the Weir 1921**
70449
The photographer is positioned on the south-east corner of Mill Meadows Island looking north to Boatslide Weir Bridge with its rustic-style balustrades. The smaller bridge to the right crosses the old boat slide, a weir bypass for rowing boats, an exciting and brief run down rollers from the upper river to the lower, and once common on the River Thames. It survives virtually intact today, but disused.

◄ **The Weir 1921** 70450
Frith's photographer has moved beyond Boatslide Weir Bridge to the bank to look at the weir itself. The chains on posts are still here to protect rowers from the hazards of the weir. Beyond the boats is the north bank of the river, and behind the trees is the large Russell Park, laid out in the late 1880s.

The Suspension Bridge 1921 70446
The rowing boat in this view is approaching the boat slide, the abutment of which is just visible on the far left. The huge weeping willow beyond is on a small island. Beyond is the Suspension Bridge linking Mill Meadow Island with Embankment Gardens at the right-hand end of the bridge.

▼ **The Suspension Bridge 1921** 70444
The hatted ladies are leaving the Suspension Bridge on the north bank, the Embankment Gardens side: casual wear in the 1920s was somewhat more formal than today. The Suspension Bridge now has a neighbour further east linking Long Island with Russell Park: this is Chris Wilkinson's 1998 Butterfly Bridge, another footbridge. Its suspension arches lean outwards like the wings of a butterfly, and it is a worthy and beautiful addition to the riverside scene.

▼ **The Promenade and the River 1921** 70443
The river banks are still just as popular today, as is 'messing around in boats'. This boomed from the late 19th century onwards, as increased leisure time reached the lower middle classes. It was as popular here on the Ouse as on the Thames, in Jerome K Jerome 'Three Men in a Boat' country. Bikes seem just as popular in this view, which looks east towards the Suspension Bridge.

▲ **The Promenade 1921**
70439
Frith's 1921 photographer has climbed the hair-pin railinged fence to look along the Embankment Gardens themselves with their neat floral beds. The quick-growing Lombardy poplars along the river promenade side of the gardens are only just over thirty years old in this view. They have long gone, along with the railings.

◀ **The Promenade 1921**

70440

A little further west, at the start of the Embankment Gardens, Frith's photographer has not quite got his focus correct. The urn on its pedestal was renewed in 1948. It has a plaque informing us that it was presented by the Indiana Limestone Co Inc to the people of Great Britain from 'The Stone City of the World', Bedford's namesake: Bedford, Indiana.

The River 1929 81731
The smart white
pleasure launch with
the awning is a frequent
sight in most of the
1920s views along the
river. At the far right is
the cut that formerly
by-passed Duck Mill's
leet, now a gated
overflow channel-cum-
lock. This viewpoint is
almost the same as
70443; it is striking
how much shorter the
young ladies' skirts
have become in the
intervening eight years.

◄ **The River 1929** 81730
In this photograph we
look west from the tip of
Mill Meadow Island
towards the
Embankment and the
north bank of the river.
The Swan Hotel is in the
distance, and the taller
building in the middle
distance is the Town and
Country Club. The
buildings on the right
have long been
demolished.

◄ **St Mary's Gardens 1929**

81736

This view is taken from the east end of Embankment Gardens, where there was a matching urn to that at their west end. This one, however, did not get renewed after World War II by the Indiana Limestone Company, and only the plinth survives. The hairpin railings were replaced after World War II by concrete block walls, but fortunately lower versions of the railings have recently replaced the ungainly blockwork.

▼ **Embankment Gardens c1955** B51027

Bedford's War Memorial was erected in Embankment Gardens around 1920; it had names subsequently added for the Second World War and the Korean War as well as the Great War. A medieval knight surmounts the tall plinth. The stone piers and chains remain, and the memorial's Portland limestone is as white as the day it was built.

◄ **The River Ouse c1955**

B51015

The riverside willows on the north bank have only recently been pollarded in this view, in which an eight rows past. The opposite bank is Long Island. The small landing stage on the right was built here to close off the boat slide, which is just behind it.

The Suspension Bridge and Embankment Gardens c1960 B51103
The inclined floral bed in the foreground survives, and is planted each year with a different theme. The concrete block walls replaced railings lost during the Second World War. The somewhat utilitarian blocks have now been replaced by low hairpin railings: a considerable improvement. The large inscription attached to the Suspension Bridge, 'Villa Bedfordia', has been removed: not many Latin-speaking sailors come this far upstream.

Newnham Bridge 1897 39961
Further east along The Embankment, Newnham Bridge crosses the north branch of the River Ouse at the south end of Tennyson Road. We are looking east from the north bank. At this time the bridge has very rustic balustrades. The scene is very different today: the bridge was rebuilt in the 1930s in concrete with cast concrete panelled parapets, and behind is the roaring road bridge of Longholme Way. This chapter's tour of the river banks is now completed, and we return to the town centre for the next chapter.

A Walk Through Bedford

St John's Street 1921 70427
Our tour starts south of the River Ouse in the area developed by
King Edward the Elder in 919 AD; it was defended by the King's
Ditch, some of which still remains after all these centuries. The
foreground buildings were demolished to make a large
roundabout, roughly where the photographer's camera is
located. The church tower on the right is St John's, originally the
chapel to St John's Hospital, whose 13th-century core survives
nearby. In the 17th century it became the rectory, St John's
House, where John Bunyan 'sought spiritual help' from John
Gifford, the vicar, in the 1650s.

**High Street
from the Bridge 1921**
70425
Moving northwards, we cross the Ouse bridge, with the High Street ahead. The buildings on the left of the mid 19th-century, and the stucco one on the right, Murfett Brothers, Motor Agents, have been demolished. The former has not been replaced, and the latter is now the 1960s Swan House. Out of picture to the right is the Swan Hotel. The girls certainly would not wheel their bikes in the middle of the road in the 21st century. Note the open-topped bus and the motor cars on the right.

◀ **St Paul's Church 1897**
39939
To the right behind the Blackpool sign is the old Floral Hall, which was demolished in 1904. It was built as the town's Corn Exchange in 1849, but was felt to be too small by the 1870s, when a new grander one was built on the north side of St Paul's Square (seen in the second view of Chapter 1, No 39931). The site was not built on again, which further contributed to the opening up of the area around the Square.

◄ St Paul's Square c1955

B51020

St Paul's Square, also known as Market Place, is bounded on the west by the churchyard of St Paul. The old guild hall and numerous small market encroachment buildings were cleared away early in the 19th century by the town's Improvement Commissioners; this in effect recreated the original scale of the medieval market place. In this view, the market place is mostly a car park, with market stalls along the south side of the Square - one is visible at the left.

▼ St Paul's Church 1898

40861

St Paul's Square became very much the civic centre of the town with the Floral Hall, the Corn Exchange, the Town Hall, the Shire Hall and County Offices looking out onto the church in its central churchyard. This view is from the south-west by the Town Hall; we can see from the west front, seen on the left, that the nave and aisles are the same height, a style known as a hall church, and the interior is in consequence light and airy.

▲ The Howard Monument 1898 40860

This statue of 1890 is by perhaps England's finest Art Nouveau sculptor, Alfred Gilbert, whose sinuous, slightly disquieting style is seen at its best around the base of the pedestal. He was the sculptor of Eros in Piccadilly Circus in London. John Howard (1726-1790) lived at nearby Cardington, and was twice Mayor of Bedford and in 1773 Lord High Sheriff of the county. He was concerned with prison reform: his name lives on in the Howard League for Penal Reform.

The Square 1929
81741
A splendid array of 1920s motor cars occupy the market place in this view looking west. At the right, behind the rather fine 18th-century churchyard gate piers, is the second Corn Exchange of 1872; the pub to its right, the Orchid, was rebuilt in 1913. At the far left is the hipped roof of Waterhouse's 1881 Shire Hall.

St Paul's Church 1929 81743
This view looks south-west. The cars occupy the site of the first Corn Exchange, which became the Floral Hall after its replacement opened in 1874. After the Hall was demolished in 1904, views opened up of the north side of the church, which is dominated by its tall spire and tower, all Victorian rebuilds of 1868. Indeed, much of the nave was also rebuilt, and there is little feel of the 14th and 15th century in this over-restored town church.

St Paul's Church c1955 B51019
Inside, Bedford's chief historical treasure is the brass to Sir William
Harpur and his wife, Dame Alice. He is in the gown of an
Alderman, and he was a Lord Mayor of London. His endowment of
the Harpur School in 1566 had a profound influence on the town's
structure and history: indeed, the Harpur Trust is still flourishing.
Over-restored or not, the church makes an excellent contribution
to the townscape, and is the focus of St Paul's Square.

High Street 1921

70424

We now move northwards into the High Street. The bank on the left has its long frontage to St Paul's Square, and is now a Ladbroke's betting shop. Most of the buildings in this view survive, although some on the left made way for a 1950s Debenhams store. The bull on top of the bracket clock on the right survives. Built in 1878 as John Bull and Co, the building is now an opticians.

High Street 1921

70423

We have moved further north. The building on the far left was demolished for the 1950s Debenhams. Silver Street, between it and the Bedford Palace, is now a pedestrianised shopping street. The Palace, a cinema, was showing 'The Black Secret' in 1921; it was rebuilt in the 1960s as a four-storey block. The buildings to the right of the smart white-gloved policemen went in the 1960s.

St Cuthbert's Church 1897 39944

Diverting eastward up Mill Street, our tour reaches St Cuthbert's Church, which served the east part of the town and was possibly of Anglo-Saxon origin. Decayed and too small, it was rebuilt in 1847; the architect Woodruffe chose the Norman style, which enjoyed a brief vogue before the Gothic Revival triumphed everywhere in Victorian England. Aisles were added in 1865. Apart from the loss of some railings, little in this view from the north-west has changed, although it is now a Polish Roman Catholic Church serving Bedford's quite sizeable Polish community.

High Street 1929 81740

At the top of the High Street, the photographer looks south. The Lime Street/Lurke Street junction is beyond the Swan Hotel's handcart. The Midland Bank with its Ionic half-columns was demolished in the 1970s; the replacement building is now a pub called The Banker's Draft. Barclays lies beyond, also in the stone-faced dignified classical dress beloved of 1920s bankers. Most of the High Street buildings survive, but without the splendid Victorian and Edwardian shopfronts. The Bear, modernised about 1900, also remains, its glazed tiles now painted.

St Peter's Square c1955 B51061
At the north end of the High Street is St Peter's Green, a large
triangular open space, with the church on the north side. St Peter's
Street is on the right. Behind the photographer, Dame Alice Street
passes the Harpur Almshouses, a long row of brick cottages in the
Tudor style thought suitable for such buildings, erected by the
Harpur Trust in 1806 but refronted in 1890.

The Bunyan Statue and St Peter's Church 1921 70428
In this splendidly evocative view from the High Street/St Peter's Street/Dame Alice Street junction, the photographer looks north along the Broadway towards the leafy De Parys Avenue, past the policeman on points duty. Beyond is the Biggleswade bus, and to the left is the taxi rank with the cabmen's shelter behind it. The lime trees alongside the Bunyan Statue have gone, and the church is more visible today.

The Bunyan Statue 1898 40857
This statue of one of Bedfordshire's famous sons was made by the noted sculptor, Boehm, in 1873, and presented to the town by the then Duke of Bedford in June 1874. This is ironic in a way, for Bunyan, the author of 'The Pilgrim's Progress', had been a thorn in the flesh of the establishment in the 17th century, and was more likely to have been cast into prison by the Duke's ancestors than otherwise.

The Bunyan Statue and St Peter's Church 1898 40856

At the time of this photograph, the statue and its pier and chain railing is still crisp and fresh-looking, and the replanted limes are young. Around the plinth are bronze panels showing scenes from 'The Pilgrim's Progress', which was published in 1678 and was one of the best sellers in the English language for centuries. Bunyan was born in Elstow; after service on the Parliamentary side in the Civil War, he moved to Bedford, where his non-conformity led to spells in Bedford Gaol.

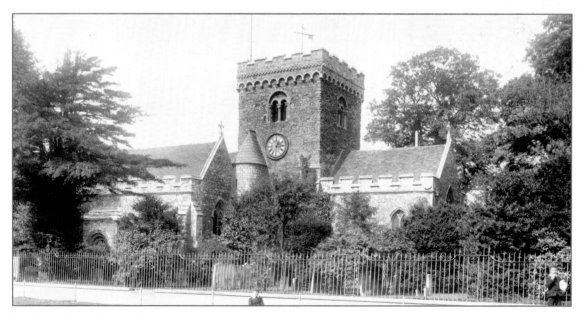

St Peter's Church 1897 39941

St Peter de Merton is of great interest, for it contains Anglo-Saxon work. The present chancel was the nave of the first church, while the tower was added after the Norman Conquest. Much of the rest of the church, the present nave and aisles to the left, are later medieval with heavy Victorian restoration. The round-arched doorway to be seen on the left was re-erected here in the 1560s; it was salvaged from the demolished church of St Peter Dunstable on Cauldwell Street south of the river.

**St Peter's Street
1921** 70426
We are looking east
along St Peter's Street,
where much on the
south side has changed.
The shop on the right
was replaced in the
1930s by neo-Georgian
offices, Royal
Chambers, and beyond
the gabled building,
now the Bedfordshire
Probation Service,
several buildings made
way for the Granada
Cinema in 1934. This
was demolished in
1990 and replaced by a
supermarket. On the
left, behind the trees, is
the south entrance to
Bedford School; the
gates bear the
inscription 'Floreat
Schola Bedfordiensis'.

▼ **De Parys Avenue 1897** 39949

Taken from the west edge of St Peter's Green, this view looks north up the long avenue towards Bedford Park. This is an early view, with the lime trees little over ten years old. Large villas in gardens lined the road; it was one of Bedford's most select areas, and was named after Robert de Parys, who had founded St John's Hospital in the late 12th century. Note the cadet resplendent in his scarlet uniform and rakishly angled pill-box hat.

▼ **De Parys Avenue 1921** 70429

Here we see the well-treed street looking more mature; the photographer is looking south back towards the town centre. It was truly a sylvan approach to Bedford Park. On the left are typical late Victorian houses; the one on the far left, No 67, is now the Bedford School Study Centre. The houses on this side back onto the playing fields of Bedford School. Only at the far end, at the Tavistock Street junction, have any Victorian houses been lost - they were replaced by a four-storey block of flats in the 1970s.

▲ **Bedford Park c1960**
B51077

The 1880s was a decade of civic pride and numerous initiatives, many during the mayorships of the vigorous Joshua Hawkins. At the end of the smart De Parys Avenue, Bedford Park was laid out to designs by the noted park designers William Barron and Sons from Derby in 1883 during Hawkins' first mayoralty. They planted over 18,000 trees and shrubs, and buildings were steadily added: pavilions and a cafe, seen in this view, and in 1903 a bandstand. The foreground is now a football pitch, where boys teams are urged on by roaring, fanatical fathers from the touchline.

◀ **Bedford Park
Entrance Gates 1921**
70430
The West Lodge and
Gates are at the head of
De Parys Avenue. The
gates were presented to
the town by the Duke of
Bedford, and the park
was opened by his
eldest son, the Marquess
of Tavistock, in July 1888
during Joshua Hawkins'
fourth mayoralty. The
gates are high-quality
ironwork, while the
stone and brick piers
carry inscription plaques
commemorating this
formal opening after five
years of hard work
creating the park. It is
still a wonderful asset for
the town and immensely
popular.

Bedford Park, The Swimming Pool c1960 B51081
From the start, sports were catered for to invigorate the lungs and hearts of Bedford's citizens, particularly those in the artisan terraces south-west of the park. Indeed, by 1900 there were rugby and football clubs in the town, while on the river Bedford Rowing Club was formed in 1886 and an annual regatta organised. Back in the park, as in so many other parks in England, an open-air swimming pool was built in the 1950s. Now in the pampered modern era it has been roofed in and expanded as The Robinson Pool.

The Park, Putnoe c1960 B51092
Beyond the route suggested in this chapter, which finishes at Bedford Park, the 1950s and 1960s expansion of Bedford to the east was well planned with parks, shopping parades and schools - many of the schools are highly regarded in architectural circles. The population of the town doubled between 1911 and 1981. The fields of Putnoe Farm were developed in the 1950s: here we look north-west from the shopping parade towards Braeside across Bowhill and the park, here in its infancy but now well treed and attractive.

A Tour To The West of Bedford

Clapham, The Village c1905 C22901

Three miles north-west of Bedford town centre, Clapham is a village whose situation on the A6 has not treated it kindly: it has lost many of the older buildings in recent years, including the thatched cottage in the middle distance, which has been rebuilt and is now Vesuvio Italian restaurant. The 1890s working men's club on the right is now disfigured by a large 1960s flat-roofed extension. The main glory of Clapham is the parish church, up a lane to the left, whose 60-foot Anglo-Saxon tower is topped by a further 25 feet of Norman work.

▼ Biddenham, The Church 1897 39962

Across the Great Ouse we reach Biddenham, now virtually joined to Bedford by housing estates. At the end of a lane near the Ouse the parish church is grouped with Church Farm. The ivy has long gone from the Early English Gothic 13th-century tower surmounted by the battlemented 15th-century bell stage and leaded spirelet. The young cedar in the foreground is now over 60 feet high, and obscures this view of the church.

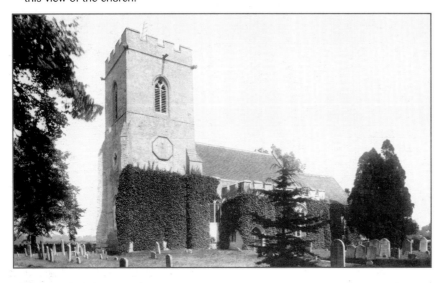

▼ Bromham, The Bridge 1897 39963

The attractive village of Bromham is now by-passed, so the old bridge over the Great Ouse is mercifully much quieter than it was a few years ago. From the south-west side we glimpse Bromham Mill and its leet beyond, now a restored and working watermill. The bridge has 26 arches, some of which date back to the 13th century, but it was substantially rebuilt in 1813. In 1902-1906, after this view was taken, the parapets were entirely renewed; this time refuges were added jutting out over the water to protect pedestrians.

▲ Turvey
The Village 1897 39970

Further along the Northampton road, another partly medieval bridge takes us out of the county over the River Great Ouse. Turvey village owes its character to estate building, much of it by the Higgins family, whose Castle Ashby-style mausoleum of about 1847 is in the churchyard. The tall terraced cottages on the right are in their simpler vernacular style, while the school and halls are Tudor style, with stone mullioned and transomed windows.

◄ **Turvey, The Three Cranes Hotel c1955** T90006

Off a northward loop from the main road is the Three Cranes, again in the estate style with leaded windows and some timber framing. Beyond is the stables and coach-house, stone fronted to the road with medieval-style buttresses and with brick side elevations. To the right, out of picture, is the drive to Turvey House; further right is the parish church, over-restored but with a superb 16th-century collection of Mordaunt family monuments.

◄ **Ampthill, Market Place c1955** A158028
This view looks south down Dunstable Street from Market Place; the Moot Hall is on the right with its slender iron-glazed casements. Its ground storey is now a surveyor and estate agents, no longer a newsagent and tobacconist. The three-storey building with painted architraved frames to the rows of sash windows is the early 18th-century White Hart, and beyond is a pedimented neo-Georgian 1930s Barclays Bank.

Ampthill, Market Place c1960

A158070

Heading south-east through winding country lanes, our short tour reaches Ampthill. The Market Place is dominated by the Moot Hall, rebuilt by the Bedford Estate in 1852 in Jacobethan style with the re-used clock cupola from the 18th-century predecessor bursting from the roof in a bizarre out-of-scale way. To the right is the water pump obelisk erected in 1756 by the Earl of Upper Ossory (an Irish title), who also demolished buildings that had encroached into the market place.

Ampthill, Woburn Street c1955

A158032

Woburn Street enters Market Place from the west and has more vernacular houses and cottages along each side. Sandhill House, on the far left, is an attractive earlier 19th-century house in villa style with bracketed eaves and a shallow slate roof. On the right is the sign for the Queen's Head pub, the queen being Henry VIII's first wife, Catherine of Aragon, who lived in Ampthill during her divorce in the early 1530s.

Ampthill, St Andrew's Church c1955

A158039

Going east from Market Place along Church Street, we reach the small square with the brown stone church on its north side, a curiously villagey one for a town. On the left is the cliff-like Dynevor House, with 1725 on the rainwater hopper-heads, three storeys of box sashes and a corniced parapet. No 36a on the right is late Georgian, while the Feoffee almshouses are late 16th-century timber-framed under the render.

◄ **Houghton Conquest Houghton House 1897** 399

This view of the ruinous west front of John Bunyan's 'Palace Beautiful' atop the 'Hill of Difficulty' shows why historia are excited by the building. It classical features: in this view see the Tuscan colonnaded loggia, which originally had tw further storeys of loggias. Thi design was extremely advanc for England, and led to its be attributed to Inigo Jones, the King's architect, on no basis all. Now the roofless romanti ruin stands where once stoo the mansion of the 'fair, and wise and good'.

◀ Houghton Conquest
Houghton House 1897 39965

A mile or so north of Ampthill, we divert right to visit the ruins of Houghton House. It looks out from the escarpment of the Greensand Ridge across the plain of central Bedfordshire through which the Great Ouse meanders. It was built from about 1615 in brick with stone dressings for the Countess of Pembroke, the sister of the Elizabethan poet and soldier Sir Philip Sidney. It was occupied from 1767 by the Earl of Upper Ossory, who had provided Ampthill with the obelisk water pump. Sad to say, the house was largely dismantled by the Duke of Bedford in 1794.

▼ Elstow
The Priory Church 1897 39969

Long before John Bunyan was born in the village, the son of a brazier or tinker, Elstow was known for its Benedictine nunnery founded in about 1075. The present church is the nave of the priory; the chancel and transepts were demolished after the Dissolution of the Monasteries by the new owners, the Radcliffes. The nave is partly Norman with 13th-century west bays, and there is, unusually, a detached 15th-century bell tower. To the far left are the ivy-clad remains of Hillersden Hall, a Jacobean E-plan mansion with the church as the north wing.

◀ Elstow
The Swan Inn 1921 70452

East of the church and the Moot Hall, a jettied timber-framed building of about 1500, standing in its green, is the main north-south village road, the High Street. Most of the village was owned by the Whitbread family, including these rows of 16th-century timber-framed cottages. Those on the left were sold to the Bedford Borough Council for £1 in 1974 and restored. The roughcast was stripped and the timbers exposed, and new housing was built behind in Bunyans Mead. The Swan is still an inn and virtually unchanged now.

Elstow, The Village 1897 39966
We are north of the junction with West End. This view, looking
south along High Street, has greatly changed: the thatched
cottages have been demolished, and modern housing has been
built on the right. Beyond the left-hand cottage the Bunyan
Memorial Hall was built in Arts and Crafts style in 1910, and at the
far left is the bell-cote of Elstow Lower School, built in 1873. The
High Street is a dead end now, cut off by modern roads.

A Tour to the East of Bedford

Eynesbury, St Mary Street 1897 39994
For our second brief tour from Bedford, we head north-east to St
Neots and Eynesbury, both actually in Huntingdonshire.
Eynesbury very much plays second fiddle to St Neots, from
which it is separated only by the Hen Brook. Indeed, in this view
the superb early 16th-century pinnacled church tower belongs to
St Mary's Church in St Neots. Eynesbury's rather humbler parish
church is behind the photographer. Most of the houses on the
left survive, although the leaded casements have been replaced.

▼ Blunham, The Hill and the Square 1968 B295013

Firmly back in Bedfordshire and heading south, our route passes through Blunham, a most attractive village, where the poet John Donne was rector from 1622 until his death in 1632, although he was also Dean of St Paul's. This view gives a good idea of the village centre: the former inn, The Ragged Staff, is by the telephone pole, and the thatched cottage opposite, The Ovens, is dated 1699. The foreground cottage has a late 16th-century chimney, but was refronted in the 19th century.

▼ Sandy, Girtford Bridge 1925 77229

Moving south we cross the River Ivel by the Girtford Bridge to reach the town of Sandy on the Great North Road, the A1. The bridge is built in greensand stone, which in Bedfordshire is actually dark brown owing to a high iron content in the rock. The bridge is late 18th-century, but the central date plaque seen here from the north-east bank on the Sandy side of the river is illegible. To the right is the garden of Ivel Cottage.

▲ Sandy, Bedford Road 19
77225

Sandy was originally a mo
Roman settlement on the
road between St Albans a
Godmanchester; in the 18
century the town became
important for its coaching
servicing the Great North
However, it is a somewhat
town, and the market squa
distinct disappointment. H
little further north up High
we look west along Bedfor
The late 19th-century tow
on the left. By 1925 it was
Astor Cinema, and is now
Roundabout Club, for ther
now a roundabout roughly
the photographer is standi

◀ **Sandy, The Railway Station 1925**
77231
This view is looking down from the road bridge; things have changed greatly at Sandy. The line on the left, beyond the trees, is the London and North Western Railway Cambridge to Bletchley line that was closed in 1968. The right-hand station is the Great Northern line, later the LNER, and its station buildings largely remain. The island platform and the LNWR station in the background were removed: there are now four tracks with overhead electric supply lines for the high-speed East Coast Main Line trains, which thunder through on their way to York and Edinburgh.

Biggleswade ▶
The Market Place
1925 77215
Three miles south of
Sandy we reach
Biggleswade, now by-
passed by the A1. It is a
town of considerable
antiquity with a large
triangular market place,
partly encroached by
later buildings. In the
distance is the Town
Hall, which was designed
by John Wing of Bedford
and built in 1844. The
building with the parapet
and tall chimney on the
left is the 1565 Market
Hall, refaced in 19th-
century render.

◀ **Biggleswade Market Square c1955**
B93014
On a busy market day the former Market House is partly concealed. It was rebuilt in 1937 with fake timber-framing applied to the outside, but it did re-use the original 1565 roof timbers. At the right is John Wing's Town Hall, which cost £80; it was in public use until 1922. The tall pedimented building to the left in hot red brick and terra cotta, dated 1912, is Georges Hall Liberal Club.

Biggleswade, The Market Place c1955 B93049
Here the photographer looks west from the Town Hall, and we can see the extensive encroachment onto the market place. Its Royal charter was confirmed as long ago as 1227. All the central buildings occupy part of the original market place, which was bounded by the buildings at the far right and left. In the distance is the parish church. On the right is where the Great Fire of Biggleswade started in 1786, so many of the buildings are later than that date.

Biggleswade, Shortmead Street 1925 77216
The photographer is looking east from the top of High Street, where there is now a roundabout, with the churchyard walls and lime trees on the left. The wall and railings have now gone. Apart from the White Horse, little on the right side of Shortmead Street survives. The corner of the building on the far left is a good timber-framed house with a jettied east front facing the church; both it and the church escaped the 1786 Great Fire.

Sutton, The Pack-Horse Bridge c1960 S795072
East of Sandy, the small village of Sutton is distinguished by its narrow medieval pack-horse bridge which took pedlars and carriers' pack ponies dry-shod past the ford, which is still in use today. There are cutwaters on the other side of the bridge with refuges; the cutwaters, like the bows of ships in shape, always face upstream. The stream eventually feeds into the Ivel. This brown sandstone bridge is an interesting survival, with much of its fabric 13th-century.

Shefford, North Bridge Street 1951 S378007
Once an important market town, Shefford was blighted this century by through traffic; its central T-junction was a bottleneck until the town was recently by-passed. Here we look south down North Bridge Street towards that junction with High Street. On the left is Porch House, a heavily-restored 16th-century house, now a bank, with the pavement passing through its ground floor. To the right is W Caton & Sons, Wine and Spirit Merchants, as it says in faded paintwork on the gable of this 1881 building.

Old Warden, The Church and Thatched Cottage c1955 0124001
Old Warden is best known nowadays for the Shuttleworth Collection of vintage aircraft and other vehicles. Since 1690 the estate has been owned by two families, the Ongleys until 1871, then the Shuttleworths, who established the Shuttleworth Trust to run things after World War II. The 'cottage orne' thatched cottages are earlier 19th-century. The whole village is similarly picturesque, although the church is medieval.

Cardington, The RAF Base c1955 C325013
We conclude the tour with another reference to manned flight, in this case airships. These gigantic sheds, originally painted black, were built to house airships: one was built in 1917 and extended to house R100, the other was built in 1927 for R101. The size is stupendous: 812 feet long, 390 feet wide and 180 feet high. Unfortunately, R101 crashed in 1930, and airship production stopped. The Short Brothers built the sheds, the administration blocks and a workers' village called Shortstown. It became an RAF base in 1936, but is no longer so and the huts have been demolished.

Index

Bedford Grammar School
21, 22–23

Bedford Park 68–69, 70

Boatslide Weir Bridge 36–37

Bridge 26, 27, 28, 29, 30–31 48–49

Bunyan Statue 62–63, 64, 65

Corn Exchange 20–21

County Schools 23

De Parys Avenue 68, 70

Embankment 31, 45

Embankment Gardens 44–45, 46

Girls School 22

Harpur Schools 20

High Street 48–49, 56–57, 58–59, 60

Howard Monument 51

Infirmary 23

Newnham Bridge 46

Ouse 24–25, 26, 27, 28–29
30–31, 32–33, 34, 36–37, 38–39
40, 42–43, 44, 45

Promenade 30, 34–35, 40–41

St Cuthbert's Church 60

St John's Street 47

St Mary's Gardens 44–45

St Pauls Church 50, 51, 52–53, 54, 55

St Pauls Square 50–51, 52–53

St Peters Church 62–63, 65

St Peters Square 61

St Peters Street 66–67

Suspension Bridge 34, 38–39 40, 46

Swan Hotel 27

Town Hall 18–19

Weir 36–37

Ampthill 74–75

Biddenham 72

Biggleswade 82–83, 84

Blunham 80

Bromham 72

Cardington 86

Clapham 71

Elstow 77, 78

Eynesbury 79

Houghton Conquest 76–77

Old Warden 86

Sandy 80–81

Shefford 85

Sutton 85

Turvey 72–73

Frith Book Co Titles

www.frithbook.co.uk

The Frith Book Company publishes over 100 new titles each year. A selection of those currently available are listed below. For latest catalogue please contact Frith Book Co.

Town Books 96pp, 100 photos. County and Themed Books 128pp, 150 photos (unless specified). All titles hardback laminated case and jacket except those indicated pb (paperback)

Around Aylesbury (pb)	1-85937-227-9	£9.99	Down the Thames	1-85937-121-3	£14.99
Around Bakewell	1-85937-113-2	£12.99	Around Dublin	1-85937-058-6	£12.99
Around Barnstaple	1-85937-084-5	£12.99	Around Dublin (pb)	1-85937-	£9.99
Around Bath	1-85937-097-7	£12.99	East Anglia (pb)	1-85937-265-1	£9.99
Berkshire (pb)	1-85937-191-4	£9.99	East London	1-85937-080-2	£14.99
Around Blackpool	1-85937-049-7	£12.99	East Sussex	1-85937-130-2	£14.99
Around Bognor Regis	1-85937-055-1	£12.99	Around Eastbourne	1-85937-061-6	£12.99
Around Bournemouth	1-85937-067-5	£12.99	Edinburgh (pb)	1-85937-193-0	£8.99
Around Bradford (pb)	1-85937-204-x	£9.99	English Castles	1-85937-078-0	£14.99
Brighton (pb)	1-85937-192-2	£8.99	English Country Houses	1-85937-161-2	£17.99
British Life A Century Ago	1-85937-103-5	£17.99	Around Exeter	1-85937-126-4	£12.99
British Life A Century Ago (pb)	1-85937-213-9	£9.99	Exmoor	1-85937-132-9	£14.99
Buckinghamshire (pb)	1-85937-200-7	£9.99	Around Falmouth	1-85937-066-7	£12.99
Camberley (pb)	1-85937-222-8	£9.99	Folkestone	1-85937-124-8	£9.99
Around Cambridge	1-85937-092-6	£12.99	Gloucestershire	1-85937-102-7	£14.99
Cambridgeshire	1-85937-086-1	£14.99	Around Great Yarmouth	1-85937-085-3	£12.99
Canals and Waterways	1-85937-129-9	£17.99	Greater Manchester (pb)	1-85937-266-x	£9.99
Cardiff (pb)	1-85937-093-4	£9.99	Around Guildford	1-85937-117-5	£12.99
Carmarthenshire	1-85937-216-3	£14.99	Around Harrogate	1-85937-112-4	£12.99
Cheltenham (pb)	1-85937-095-0	£9.99	Hastings & Bexhill (pb)	1-85937-131-0	£9.99
Around Chester	1-85937-090-x	£12.99	Helston (pb)	1-85937-214-7	£9.99
Around Chichester	1-85937-089-6	£12.99	Herefordshire	1-85937-174-4	£14.99
Around Chichester (pb)	1-85937-228-7	£9.99	Around Horsham	1-85937-127-2	£12.99
Churches of Berkshire	1-85937-170-1	£17.99	Humberside	1-85937-215-5	£14.99
Churches of Dorset	1-85937-172-8	£17.99	Around Ipswich	1-85937-133-7	£12.99
Colchester (pb)	1-85937-188-4	£8.99	Ireland (pb)	1-85937-181-7	£9.99
Cornish Coast	1-85937-163-9	£14.99	Isle of Man	1-85937-065-9	£14.99
Cornwall	1-85937-054-3	£14.99	Isle of Wight	1-85937-114-0	£14.99
Cornwall (pb)	1-85937-229-5	£9.99	Kent (pb)	1-85937-189-2	£9.99
Cotswolds (pb)	1-85937-	£9.99	Kent Living Memories	1-85937-125-6	£14.99
County Durham	1-85937-123-x	£14.99	Lancaster, Morecombe & Heysham (pb)		
Cumbria	1-85937-101-9	£14.99		1-85937-233-3	£9.99
Dartmoor	1-85937-145-0	£14.99	Leeds (pb)	1-85937-202-3	£9.99
Derbyshire (pb)	1-85937-196-5	£9.99	Around Leicester	1-85937-073-x	£12.99
Devon	1-85937-052-7	£14.99	Leicestershire (pb)	1-85937-185-x	£9.99
Dorset	1-85937-075-6	£14.99	Around Lincoln	1-85937-111-6	£12.99
Dorset Coast	1-85937-062-4	£14.99	Lincolnshire	1-85937-135-3	£14.99
Dorset Living Memories	1-85937-210-4	£14.99	London (pb)	1-85937-183-3	£9.99
Down the Severn	1-85937-118-3	£14.99	Ludlow (pb)	1-85937-176-0	£9.99

Available from your local bookshop or from the publisher

Frith Book Co Titles (continued)

Around Maidstone	1-85937-056-x	£12.99	South Devon Living Memories	1-85937-168-x	£14.99
Manchester (pb)	1-85937-198-1	£9.99	Staffordshire (96pp)	1-85937-047-0	£12.99
Peterborough (pb)	1-85937-219-8	£9.99	Stone Circles & Ancient Monuments		
Piers	1-85937-237-6	£17.99		1-85937-143-4	£17.99
New Forest	1-85937-128-0	£14.99	Around Stratford upon Avon	1-85937-098-5	£12.99
Around Newark	1-85937-105-1	£12.99	Suffolk (pb)	1-85937-221-x	£9.99
Around Newquay	1-85937-140-x	£12.99	Surrey (pb)	1-85937-	
Norfolk (pb)	1-85937-195-7	£9.99	Sussex (pb)	1-85937-184-1	£9.99
North Devon Coast	1-85937-146-9	£14.99	Swansea (pb)	1-85937-167-1	£9.99
North Yorks (pb)	1-85937-236-8	£9.99	Tees Valley & Cleveland	1-85937-211-2	£14.99
Norwich (pb)	1-85937-194-9	£8.99	Thanet (pb)	1-85937-116-7	£9.99
Around Nottingham	1-85937-060-8	£12.99	Tiverton (pb)	1-85937-178-7	£9.99
Nottinghamshire (pb)	1-85937-187-6	£9.99	Around Torbay	1-85937-063-2	£12.99
Around Oxford	1-85937-096-9	£12.99	Around Truro	1-85937-147-7	£12.99
Peak District	1-85937-100-0	£14.99	Victorian & Edwardian Kent	1-85937-149-3	£14.99
Around Penzance	1-85937-069-1	£12.99	Victorian & Edwardian Maritime Album		
Around Plymouth	1-85937-119-1	£12.99		1-85937-144-2	£17.99
Norfolk Living Memories	1-85937-217-1	£14.99	Victorian and Edwardian Sussex		
North Yorks (pb)	1-85937-236-8	£9.99		1-85937-157-4	£14.99
Preston (pb)	1-85937-212-0	£9.99	Victorian & Edwardian Yorkshire	1-85937-154-x	£14.99
Reading (pb)	1-85937-238-4	£9.99	Victorian Seaside	1-85937-159-0	£17.99
Salisbury (pb)	1-85937-239-2	£9.99	Warwickshire (pb)	1-85937-203-1	£9.99
Around St Ives	1-85937-068-3	£12.99	West Midlands	1-85937-109-4	£14.99
Around Scarborough	1-85937-104-3	£12.99	West Sussex	1-85937-148-5	£14.99
Scotland (pb)	1-85937-182-5	£9.99	West Yorkshire (pb)	1-85937-201-5	£9.99
Around Sevenoaks and Tonbridge	1-85937-057-8	£12.99	Weymouth (pb)	1-85937-209-0	£9.99
Somerset	1-85937-153-1	£14.99	Wiltshire Living Memories	1-85937-245-7	£14.99
South Hams	1-85937-220-1	£14.99	Around Winchester	1-85937-139-6	£12.99
Around Southampton	1-85937-088-8	£12.99	Windmills & Watermills	1-85937-242-2	£17.99
Around Southport	1-85937-106-x	£12.99	Worcestershire	1-85937-152-3	£14.99
Around Shrewsbury	1-85937-110-8	£12.99	York (pb)	1-85937-199-x	£9.99
Shropshire	1-85937-083-7	£14.99	Yorkshire Living Memories	1-85937-166-3	£14.99
South Devon Coast	1-85937-107-8	£14.99			

Frith Book Co titles available 2001

Lake District (pb)	1-85937-275-9	£9.99	Luton (pb)	1-85937-235-x	£9.99
Sussex (pb)	1-85937-184-1	£9.99	Cheshire (pb)	1-85937-271-6	£9.99
Northumberland and Tyne & Wear (pb)			Peak District (pb)	1-85937-280-5	£9.99
	1-85937-281-3	£9.99	Dorset (pb)	1-85937-269-4	£9.99
Devon (pb)	1-85937-297-x	£9.99	Liverpool and Merseyside (pb)	1-85937-234-1	£9.99
Bedford (pb)	1-85937-205-8	£9.99	Surrey (pb)	1-85937-081-0	£9.99
Down the Thames (pb)	1-85937-278-3	£9.99	Buckinghamshire (pb)	1-85937-200-7	£9.99
Hereford (pb)	1-85937-175-2	£9.99	Heart of Lancashire (pb)	1-85937-197-3	£9.99
Brighton (pb)	1-85937-192-2	£9.99			

See Frith books on the internet www.frithbook.co.uk

FRITH PRODUCTS & SERVICES

Francis Frith would doubtless be pleased to know that the pioneering publishing venture he started in 1860 still continues today. A hundred and forty years later, The Francis Frith Collection continues in the same innovative tradition and is now one of the foremost publishers of vintage photographs in the world. Some of the current activities include:

Interior Decoration

Today Frith's photographs can be seen framed and as giant wall murals in thousands of pubs, restaurants, hotels, banks, retail stores and other public buildings throughout the country. In every case they enhance the unique local atmosphere of the places they depict and provide reminders of gentler days in an increasingly busy and frenetic world.

Product Promotions

Frith products are used by many major companies to promote the sales of their own products or to reinforce their own history and heritage. Frith promotions have been used by Hovis bread, Courage beers, Scots Porage Oats, Colman's mustard, Cadbury's foods, Mellow Birds coffee, Dunhill pipe tobacco, Guinness, and Bulmer's Cider.

Genealogy and Family History

As the interest in family history and roots grows world-wide, more and more people are turning to Frith's photographs of Great Britain for images of the towns, villages and streets where their ancestors lived; and, of course, photographs of the churches and chapels where their ancestors were christened, married and buried are an essential part of every genealogy tree and family album.

Frith Products

All Frith photographs are available Framed or just as Mounted Prints and Posters (size 23 x 16 inches). These may be ordered from the address below. From time to time other products - Address Books, Calendars, Table Mats, etc - are available.

The Internet

Already twenty thousand Frith photographs can be viewed and purchased on the internet. By the end of the year 2000 some 60,000 Frith photographs will be available on the internet. The number of sites is constantly expanding, each focussing on different products and services from the Collection.
The main Frith sites are listed below.
www.francisfrith.co.uk
www.frithbook.co.uk

See the complete list of Frith Books at:
www.frithbook.co.uk
This web site is regularly updated with the latest list of publications from the Frith Book Company. If you wish to buy books relating to another part of the country that your local bookshop does not stock, you may purchase on-line.

For further information, trade, or author enquiries please contact us at the address below:
The Francis Frith Collection, Frith's Barn, Teffont, Salisbury, Wiltshire, England SP3 5QP.
Tel: +44 (0)1722 716 376 Fax: +44 (0)1722 716 881 Email: uksales@francisfrith.co.uk

---

See Frith books on the internet www.frithbook.co.uk

TO RECEIVE YOUR FREE MOUNTED PRINT

Mounted Print
Overall size 14 x 11 inches

Cut out this Voucher and return it with your remittance for £1.50 to cover postage and handling, to UK addresses. For overseas addresses please include £4.00 post and handling. Choose any photograph included in this book. Your SEPIA print will be A4 in size, and mounted in a cream mount with burgundy rule lines, overall size 14 x 11 inches.

Order additional Mounted Prints at HALF PRICE (only £7.49 each*)

If there are further pictures you would like to order, possibly as gifts for friends and family, purchase them at half price (no additional postage and handling required).

Have your Mounted Prints framed*

For an additional £14.95 per print you can have your chosen Mounted Print framed in an elegant polished wood and gilt moulding, overall size 16 x 13 inches (no additional postage and handling required).

> *** IMPORTANT!**
> These special prices are only available if ordered using the original voucher on this page (no copies permitted) and at the same time as your free Mounted Print, for delivery to the same address

Frith Collectors' Guild

From time to time we publish a magazine of news and stories about Frith photographs and further special offers of Frith products. If you would like 12 months FREE membership, please return this form.

Send completed forms to:
The Francis Frith Collection, Frith's Barn, Teffont, Salisbury, Wiltshire SP3 5QP

Voucher for FREE and Reduced Price Frith Prints

Picture no.	Page number	Qty	Mounted @ £7.49	Framed + £14.95	Total Cost
		1	**Free of charge***	£	£
			£7.49	£	£
			£7.49	£	£
			£7.49	£	£
			£7.49	£	£
			£7.49	£	£

Please allow 28 days for delivery   *** Post & handling**   **£1.50**

Book Title . . . .   **Total Order Cost**   **£**

Please do not photocopy this voucher. Only the original is valid, so please cut it out and return it to us.

I enclose a cheque / postal order for £ . . . .
made payable to 'The Francis Frith Collection'
OR please debit my Mastercard / Visa / Switch / Amex card
(credit cards please on all overseas orders)

Number . . . .

Issue No (Switch only) . . . . .Valid from (Amex/Switch) . . . .

Expires . . . . Signature . . . .

Name Mr/Mrs/Ms . . . .

Address . . . .

. . . .

. . . . Postcode . . . .

Daytime Tel No . . . .   Valid to 31/12/02

The Francis Frith Collectors' Guild

Please enrol me as a member for 12 months free of charge.

Name Mr/Mrs/Ms . . . .

Address . . . .

. . . .

. . . . Postcode . . . .

Free Print - see overleaf